James A

By United Library

https://campsite.bio/unitedlibrary

Table of Contents

Disclaimer

This biography book is a work of nonfiction based on the public life of a famous person. The author has used publicly available information to create this work. While the author has thoroughly researched the subject and attempted to depict it accurately, it is not meant to be an exhaustive study of the subject. The views expressed in this book are those of the author alone and do not necessarily reflect those of any organization associated with the subject. This book should not be taken as an endorsement, legal advice, or any other form of professional advice. This book was written for entertainment purposes only.

Introduction

Discover the fascinating life of James A. Garfield, the twentieth President of the United States, whose legacy transcends his brief tenure in the White House. From his humble beginnings in a log cabin to his rise as a political and military leader, Garfield was a key figure in 19th-century American history.

Garfield demonstrated his talent both in politics and in the military, serving in Congress and as a general in the American Civil War. His unwavering support for the gold standard and his reputation as a gifted orator earned him the respect of his colleagues and the confidence of the American people.

As president, Garfield faced major challenges, from fighting corruption in the postal service to defending the civil rights of African-Americans. His tragic death at the hands of a deranged assassin shocked the nation and brought a premature end to his promising presidency.

Through this captivating biography, you'll discover in depth the life and legacy of a man who dedicated his life to serving his country, and left an indelible mark on American history.

Immerse yourself in history with this fascinating biography by James A. Garfield. Order it today!

James A. Garfield

James Abram Garfield, born November 19, 1831 in Orange, Ohio, and assassinated September 19, 1881 in Elberon, New Jersey, was an American statesman and 20th President of the United States.

After nine consecutive elections to the U.S. House of Representatives in Ohio between 1863 and 1881, Garfield became President on the Republican ticket. His term, cut short by his assassination, was marked by a controversial resurgence of presidential authority over Senate precedence in federal appointments, a revival of American naval power, the elimination of corruption in the postal service and the appointment of several African-Americans to high federal office.

Garfield grew up on a modest Ohio farm, where he was raised by his widowed mother and older brother. To finance his education, Garfield worked at a number of jobs before graduating in 1856 from Williams College in Massachusetts. A year later, he entered politics with the Republican Party, campaigning against slavery in Ohio. He married Lucretia Rudolph in 1858 and was admitted to the bar two years later, as well as being elected to the Ohio Senate between 1859 and 1861. Garfield opposed the secession of the Southern states and became a major general in the Union army, with whom he participated in the battles of Shiloh and Chickamauga. He was elected to Congress in 1862, representing Ohio's 19th district.

Throughout his long career in Congress after the Civil War, he vehemently opposed *greenbacks* and earned a reputation as a gifted orator. He is chairman of the Committees on Military Affairs and Appropriations, and a member of the Committee on Fiscal Affairs. Garfield was initially close to the views of the Radical Republicans on Reconstruction, but later favored a more flexible approach to the enforcement of civil rights for freed slaves. In 1880, the Ohio legislature elected him to the U.S. Senate; the same year, the leading Republican presidential contenders, Ulysses S. Grant, James Blaine and John Sherman, failed to rally sufficient support at the convention. Garfield became the compromise candidate for the 1880 presidential election, declining the federal Senate nomination to enter the presidential race, in which he defeated the Democratic candidate Winfield Hancock.

Garfield's presidency lasted just 200 days, from March 4, 1881, until his death on September 19, 1881, after being shot by Charles J. Guiteau on the previous July 2. Only William Henry Harrison's presidency of 31 days was shorter, and Garfield was the second of the four American presidents to be assassinated. He proposed a far-reaching reform of the civil service, which was finally enacted in 1883 by his vice-president and successor Chester A. Arthur in the form of the *Pendleton Civil Service Reform Act*.

JAMES A. GARFIELD & FAMILY.

Biography

Youth

James Garfield was born on November 19, 1831, in Cuyahoga County near present-day Orange, Ohio, the youngest of five children. His father, Abram Garfield, known locally for his wrestling activities, died when James was just 18 months old. Of Welsh descent, he was raised by his mother, Eliza Ballou, who said he "was the biggest baby I ever had and looked like a redheaded Irishman". Garfield's parents had joined the followers of Christ, and they had a profound influence on the young boy. Garfield received a rudimentary education at the village school in Orange. He knew, however, that he would need money to continue his studies.

At the age of 16, he decided to strike out on his own and turned to the sea in the hope of becoming a sailor; however, he only got a job as a laborer on a canal near Cleveland for six weeks. He fell ill and returned home, but after recovering he attended Geauga Academy, where he discovered a passion for learning. Garfield worked as a carpenter, bell ringer and janitor to finance his studies. He later said of this period: "I am sad that I was born into poverty and the chaos of childhood, 17 years passed before I found any inspiration... 17 precious years in which a boy with a father and a little money could have been fixed in various manly ways". In 1849, he accepted a teaching post that didn't suit him, and subsequently developed an aversion to what he called "job-hunting" that became, in his words, "the law of my life". In 1850 Garfield returned to the church and was baptized.

Education, marriage and starting a career

From 1851 to 1854, he studied at the Western Reserve Eclectic Institute (later renamed Hiram College) in Hiram, Ohio. At Eclectic, he became interested in the study of Greek and Latin, and began teaching. He also had the ability to write, simultaneously, in Latin with one hand and ancient Greek with the other. He made many rounds of preaching in neighboring churches, sometimes earning a dollar per service. Garfield then enrolled at Williams College in Williamstown, Massachusetts, where he joined the Delta Upsilon fraternity. Garfield was impressed by the college's president, Mark Hopkins, about whom he declared, "The ideal education is Mark Hopkins on one end of a stump and a student on the other." Garfield gained a reputation as a gifted debater and became president of the Philogian Society and editor of the *Williams Quarterly*. After a remarkable career, he graduated in 1856.

After preaching briefly at Franklin Circle Christian Church, Garfield abandoned this vocation and applied for the position of principal at Poestenkill High School in Poestenkill, New York. Unsuccessful, he returned to teach at the Eclectic Institute. He taught classical literature during the 1856-1857 academic year, before becoming principal of the Institute from 1857 to 1860; he succeeded in restoring the school's declining appeal. During this period, Garfield moved closer to the ideas of moderate Republicans, even though he was not a party man. While he didn't consider himself an abolitionist, he was opposed to slavery. After graduating, he began a career in politics, making numerous speeches in support of the Republican party and their anti-slavery cause. In 1858, an atheist and proponent of evolutionism named Denton got into a debate with him (Charles Darwin's *Origin of Species* was published the following year). The debate, which lasted over a week, was considered to have been won by Garfield.

Garfield's first love was Mary Hubbell in 1851, but the relationship lasted a year without any formal commitment. On November 11, 1858, he married Lucretia Rudolph, one of his former students. They had seven children (five sons and two daughters): Eliza Arabella Garfield (1860-1863); Harry Augustus Garfield (1863-1942); James Rudolph Garfield (1865-1950); Mary Garfield (1867-1947); Irvin M. Garfield (1870-1951); Abram Garfield (1872-1958) and Edward Garfield (1874-76). James R. Garfield also entered politics, becoming

Secretary of the Interior under President Theodore Roosevelt.

Garfield gradually lost interest in teaching and began studying law in 1859. He was admitted to the Ohio bar in 1861. Prior to his admission, he was invited to enter politics by local Republican leaders, and to run for state senator for Ohio's 26th district after the death of Cyrus Prentiss, who held that office. He was nominated by the party convention and elected state senator from 1859 to 1861. The most significant act of his tenure was the drafting of legislation to conduct the state's first geological survey to determine its mineral resources. As the nation moved closer to civil war, Garfield saw secession as inconceivable. His response was renewed zeal for the July 4, 1860 celebrations.

After Abraham Lincoln's election, Garfield was more interested in arming than negotiating, declaring, "The other states may arm themselves to the teeth, but if Ohio cleans out her rusty muskets, they say she offends her Southern brethren. I am weary of this weakness. On February 13, 1861, the newly elected President Lincoln arrived in Cincinnati by train to give a speech. Garfield noted that Lincoln was "hopelessly modest" yet had "the tone and stature of a solid, fearless man".

Military career

Under Buell's command

At the outbreak of the Civil War, Garfield was frustrated by his failure to secure an officer's position in the Union army. Ohio Governor William Dennison commissioned him to travel to Illinois to acquire arms and negotiate with the governors of Illinois and Indiana to reinforce the troops. In the summer of 1861, he was finally appointed colonel in the Union Army and given command of the 42nd Ohio Volunteer Regiment.

General Don Carlos Buell assigned Garfield the task of driving Confederate forces from eastern Kentucky in November 1861, and granted him the 18th Brigade for this campaign. In December, he left Catlettsburg, Kentucky, with the 40 and 42 Ohio infantry regiments, the 14 and 22 Kentucky regiments and the 2 Virginia cavalry. The move was uneventful until the arrival of Union forces at Paintsville, Kentucky on January 6, 1862, when Garfield's cavalry engaged the Confederates at Jenny's Creek. Garfield skillfully deployed his troops to make the enemy believe he was outnumbered, when in fact he was not. The Confederates led by Brigadier General Humphrey Marshall withdrew to Middle Creek, about 3 km from Prestonsburg on the Virginia Turnpike. Garfield attacked on January 10, 1862. At the end of the day, the Confederate soldiers retreated, but Garfield did not pursue them, retreating to Prestonburg to resupply his troops. His victories brought him recognition, and he was promoted to the rank of brigadier-general on January 11.

Garfield then commanded the 20th Ohio Brigade under Buell at the Battle of Shiloh, where his troops, delayed by bad weather, reinforced Major-General Ulysses S. Grant's units threatened by a surprise attack from Confederate General Albert S. Johnston. Grant's units threatened by a surprise attack from Confederate general Albert S. Johnston. He then served under Thomas J. Wood at the siege of Corinth in Mississippi, and took part in the pursuit of retreating Confederate forces led by the excessively cautious Major-General Henry W. Halleck. This led to the escape of General P. G. T. Beauregard and his men, and instilled in the furious Garfield a nagging distrust of training at West Point Military Academy. Garfield's 1862 military philosophy of aggressively waging war against Southern civilians was not yet accepted by Union generals. The tactic was subsequently adopted and applied in the campaigns of Generals Sherman and Sheridan.

Garfield commented on slavery in 1862: "If a man is black, whether friend or foe, it is best to keep him at a distance. It is scarcely possible that God will allow us to succeed while such enormities are being practiced." In the summer of 1862, his health took a sudden turn for the worse, and he developed jaundice and lost a lot of weight; biographer Peskin suggests that he was suffering from infectious hepatitis. Garfield had to return home, where his wife looked after him and he recovered. He returned to the army in the fall and took part in the court-martial of Fitz John Porter. Garfield was then sent to Washington to receive new orders. To his frustration, he received various temporary assignments in Florida, Virginia and South Carolina, all of which were successively cancelled. During his inactivity in Washington awaiting an assignment, Garfield spent much of his time corresponding with friends and family. An unconfirmed rumor of an extramarital affair caused some tension in his marriage, but Lucretia forgave him.

Rosecrans Chief of Staff

In the spring of 1863, Garfield returned to the front as chief of staff to General William Starke Rosecrans, commander of the Army of the Cumberland. His influence in this post was greater than expected; his prerogatives extended beyond mere communication to the management of Rosecrans' entire army. Rosecrans, a particularly energetic man, was a gifted debater and didn't hesitate to engage in verbal jousting when he couldn't sleep; in Garfield he found "the first well-educated person in the Army" and therefore the ideal candidate for endless late-night discussions. The two men became close and exchanged views on all subjects, especially religion; Rosecrans managed to soften Garfield's view of Catholicism. Garfield, with his great influence, created an intelligence corps unrivalled in the Union army. He also requested that Rosecrans replace Lieutenant-Colonels Alexander Mac Dowell Mac Cook and Thomas Leonidas Crittenden on account of their previous inefficiency. Rosecrans ignored these recommendations, with disastrous consequences at the Battle of Chickamauga. Garfield devised a campaign to pursue and trap Confederate general Braxton Bragg at Tullahoma, Tennessee. The army successfully advanced to the city, but Bragg retreated to Chattanooga. Rosecrans halted his advance and repeatedly requested reinforcements. Garfield proposed an immediate attack to his superior and devised a plan to conduct a cavalry raid behind Bragg's line, which Rosecrans approved; the raid, led by Abel Streight (en), failed partly due to bad weather. Garfield's critics went on to argue that the whole idea of the operation was wrong. To settle the continuing question of the advance, Rosecrans assembled a military council of his generals; 10 out of 15 were opposed to an advance, while Garfield had voted in favor. Nevertheless, Garfield, in an unusual move, wrote up the council's deliberations and convinced Rosecrans to resume the offensive against Bragg.

At the Battle of Chickamauga, Rosecrans issued an order intended to fill a gap in his line, but this created another. As a result, his right flank was routed. Rosecrans concluded that the battle was lost and headed for Chattanooga to establish a new line of defense. Garfield considered, however, that part of the army had held and, with Rosecrans' agreement, headed for Missionary Ridge to check on the Union forces. His hunch was correct; his ride became famous, while Rosecrans' error reinforced the criticism of his command. While Rosecrans' army had avoided complete destruction, it was trapped in Chattanooga and surrounded by Bragg's army. Garfield sent a telegram to Secretary of War Edwin M. Stanton alerting Washington that without reinforcements, the Union troops would be swept away. As a result, Lincoln and Halleck sent 20,000 men to Chattanooga by rail in less than nine days. One of Grant's first decisions upon assuming command of the western armies as *major general* was to replace Rosecrans with George H. Thomas in October 1863. Garfield was ordered to report to Washington, where he was promoted to the rank of major-general; soon afterwards he gave an unequivocal abolitionist speech in Maryland. He wasn't sure whether to return to the field or assume the Ohio representative seat he'd won in October 1862. After a discussion with

Lincoln, he decided to leave the army and join Congress. According to historian Jean Edward Smith, Grant and Garfield had had a "cautious relationship" since Grant had replaced Rosecrans with Thomas instead of Garfield at the head of the Army of the Cumberland.

Garfield confided his frustration with Rosecrans in a confidential letter to his friend, Treasury Secretary Salmon P. Chase. Garfield's detractors later used this letter, which Chase never personally made public, to portray Garfield as a traitor despite the fact that Halleck and Lincoln had shared concerns about Rosecrans' reluctance to attack and that Garfield had openly expressed his concerns with Rosecrans. Years later, Charles Anderson Dana of the *New York Sun* claimed to have sources indicating that Garfield had publicly stated that Rosecrans had fled the Chickamauga battlefield. According to biographer Peskin, the credibility of these sources and information is questionable. For historian Bruce Catton, Garfield's statements influenced the Lincoln administration in its decision to find a replacement for Rosecrans.

Congress

Election of 1862 and first mandate

While serving in the army, Garfield was approached in early 1862 by friends about political opportunities related to the redrawing of Ohio's 19 congressional district; the incumbent, John Hutchins, was indeed considered vulnerable. Garfield was conflicted; he was sure he would be more useful in Congress than on the battlefield, but he didn't want his military position to be a springboard for his political career. He expressed his willingness to serve if elected, but would not campaign for it, leaving that to others. Garfield was nominated by the Republican convention after 75 ballots. In October 1862, he defeated D.B. Woods by a large majority in the election to represent Ohio's 19th congressional district in the 38th Congress.

After the election, Garfield was anxious to get his next military assignment and went to Washington to do just that. While there, he became close to Salmon P. Chase, Lincoln's Secretary of the Treasury. Garfield joined the radical Republicans led by Chase in opposition to the moderate wing of the party represented by Lincoln and Montgomery Blair. Garfield was also frustrated by Lincoln's lack of aggressiveness in pursuing the

Confederate army, as had been the case with General George McClellan. Chase and Garfield shared the same disdain for West Point and the President, although Garfield congratulated him on the Emancipation Proclamation. Garfield also shared a negative view of General McClellan, whom he saw as the symbol of the pro-slavery, ill-tempered Democratic generals of West Point.

Garfield became fascinated with discussions of financial and economic policy in Chase's office, and these subjects became his area of expertise. Like Chase, Garfield became a staunch advocate of "honest money" supported by the gold standard and was therefore an opponent of *greenbacks*; he regretted but understood the need for a suspension of currency payments in the face of the emergency caused by the Civil War.

Although he wanted to continue his military career, Garfield reluctantly accepted his seat in Congress by resigning from his military duties in December 1863. His first daughter Eliza died that same month when she was just three years old. Although he initially took a room alone, his grief over Eliza's death prompted him to find a roommate in his colleague, Robert C. Schenck. After the end of Garfield's tenure, Lucretia moved to Washington to be with her husband, and the two never parted again.

Garfield immediately demonstrated his ability to attract the attention of the unruly House. According to one journalist, "when he rises to speak, Garfield's voice surpasses all others. All ears turn to him...His eloquence touches hearts, convinces reason and points the weak and undecided to the way forward." He was one of the most bellicose Republicans in the House, and served on the Armed Services Committee headed by Schenck and charged with urgent matters of war. Garfield aggressively defended the need for conscription, a subject avoided by many others.

Early in his term, he distinguished himself from his party on several counts: he was the only Republican to vote to end the use of bounties in the draft. He was the only Republican to vote for an end to the use of bounties in the draft, as some wealthy recruits could pay to avoid conscription, which he considered reprehensible. After numerous setbacks, Garfield, with Lincoln's support, secured passage of a conscription bill that put an end to this system. In 1864, Congress passed a bill to recreate the rank of lieutenant general. Garfield, like Thaddeus Stevens, was not in favor of this action, as the rank was intended for Grant, who had removed Rosecrans from office. In addition, the recipient would receive an advantage in a possible election against Lincoln. Garfield was, however, hesitant about supporting the President's re-election.

Garfield was sometimes close to the ideas of the Radical-Republicans, as on abolition, and considered, at the beginning of his mandate, that the leaders of the Confederacy should be stripped of their constitutional rights. He supported the confiscation of Southern plantations and even the exile or execution of Confederate leaders to prevent any return to slavery. He considered that Congress had an obligation to "determine what legislation was necessary to insure the equal treatment of all honest people, regardless of color". For the 1864 election, Garfield didn't consider Lincoln deserving of re-election, but there was no alternative: "I have no candidate for the presidency. I am a sad and unhappy spectator of events. He attended his party's convention and supported Rosecrans for the vice-presidential nomination; he was greeted by the latter's characteristic indecision and Andrew Johnson was chosen. Garfield voted with the Radical-Republicans in favor of the Wade-Davis Act (en), which excluded all parliamentarians who had participated in the Confederacy, but this was rejected by Lincoln.

Election of 1864 and second term

By the time of the 1864 House election, Garfield's partisan base had weakened due to his lack of support for Lincoln's re-election, but it strengthened when he demonstrated his traditional disdain for partisanship; he was nominated by acclamation and his re-election was assured. While he was resting after his election, Lucretia sent him a letter stating that they had been together only 20 weeks out of 57 since the beginning of his first term; he immediately decided to bring his family to Washington. As the end of the war approached, the activities of the Armed Services Committee began to slow down; this increased his weariness of partisan politics, and Garfield concentrated on his personal activities. Garfield had teamed up with Illinois Representative Ralph Plumb (en) in land speculation activities, but they met with only limited success. He joined the Philadelphia-based Phillips brothers in oil exploration, which proved moderately profitable. Garfield returned to the practice of law in 1865 to improve his personal finances.

Garfield's radicalism moderated after the end of the Civil War and Lincoln's assassination; he assumed a temporary role as conciliator between Congress and Andrew Johnson. At that time, he commented on the readmission of the Confederate States: "The burden of proof is upon them to show whether they are able to enter the Federal circle with full privileges. They must give us proof, as solid as the Holy Scriptures, that they have changed and are again worthy of our confidence." By the time Johnson's veto put an end to the Freedman's Bureau, the President had effectively come into conflict with Congress, and Garfield joined the radical camp.

With a reduced agenda on the Armed Forces Committee, Garfield entered the House Ways and Means Committee, an opportunity for him to focus on economic and financial issues. He immediately resumed his opposition to *greenbacks*, declaring "any party that turns to paper money will fall in the midst of widespread disaster and be cursed by the ruined populace". He called *greenbacks* "the printed lies of government" and became a staunch advocate of the morality and legality of payment in metal coinage and the establishment of the gold standard. This policy was contrary to his personal interests, as his investments depended on the inflation that was a consequence of *greenbacks*. His demand for a gold standard was fundamentally deflationary, and was opposed by most businessmen and politicians. For a time, Garfield seemed to be the only Ohio politician to champion the idea.

As a proponent of laissez-faire economics, he declared, "the main role of government is to keep the peace and keep out of the sunshine of the people". This vision was in stark contrast to his idea of government's role in Reconstruction. Another inconsistency in his laissez-faire philosophy was his stance on free trade, as he defended tariffs when they served to protect his district's products.

Garfield was one of three defense attorneys in the famous *Ex parte Milligan* decision handed down by the

Supreme Court in 1866. Despite his many years of legal practice, this was Garfield's first courtroom appearance. Judge Jeremiah S. Black had chosen him as a partner a year earlier, and entrusted him with the case in light of his highly regarded oratory skills. The defendants were pro-Confederate Northerners who had been found guilty and sentenced to death by a military tribunal for treason. The question was whether the defendants should have been tried in a civilian court; Garfield was victorious and immediately gained a reputation as an eminent appellate court lawyer.

Election of 1866 and third term

Despite the lure of this lucrative practice, Garfield didn't hesitate when he decided to run again in 1866 due to the urgency created by Reconstruction. The competition was tougher, as Garfield had taken positions that pushed him onto the defensive, such as conscription and tariff legislation and his involvement in the Milligan affair. The party convention nevertheless voted in his favor, and Garfield won the election by a wide margin. At the same time, the Republicans won two-thirds of the seats in Congress.

Garfield returned to Washington very glum despite his success, for he had not taken kindly to the criticism he had received during the campaign. He was also disappointed by what he saw as the crazy debates surrounding President Johnson's *impeachment.* As far as Reconstruction was concerned, he felt that Congress had been magnanimous in its offers to the South. When the old Confederates saw this as a sign of weakness and sought to exploit it with other demands, he was quite willing to reconsider them as enemies of the Union. This vision was popular in his district, and activists considered running Garfield for governor of Ohio, but he declined.

Garfield hoped that his new mandate would enable him to be appointed chairman of the Ways and Means Committee, but this was largely not the case, due to his strong positions on monetary issues, which did not reflect the consensus in the House. On the other hand, he was appointed chairman of the Armed Forces Committee, whose main task was the reorganization and reduction of the armed forces after the end of the Civil War. Garfield approved of the Senate, through the *Tenure of Office Act*, having the final say on Cabinet appointments, a position that largely evolved when he became President.

Garfield's position on the President evolved, and he defended the articles of *impeachment* against Johnson on the grounds that he had violated the *Tenure of Office Act* by dismissing Secretary of War Edwin M. Stanton. Garfield was absent from the vote because of his work as a jurist. While most Senators were convinced of Johnson's guilt, they did not want U.S. Senate President *Pro Tempore*

Benjamin Wade, a radical Republican with extreme views for the time, to become President. Garfield sensed that the senators were more interested in making speeches than in conducting a real trial. Eventually, Chief Justice Salmon P. Chase, who presided over the trial, would allow Johnson's acquittal thanks to his statements. As a result, Garfield's very close friend became a political adversary, even though he continued to follow the economic and financial visions he had learned from him. In 1868, Garfield gave a two-hour speech on monetary issues that was widely hailed as his best to date; in it, he advocated the gradual resumption of metal coinage.

Election of 1868 and fourth term

The contest for re-election was simpler in 1868 than two years earlier, as Garfield's opponents had little to criticize him for. His nomination went smoothly, and he gave more than 60 campaign speeches before being re-elected with a comfortable lead. At the same time, Grant won the presidency. From the outset, Garfield's relations with the new president were rather cool; Grant refused a nomination that Garfield had advised, and Garfield continued to harbor resentment over Rosecrans' dismissal. After housing his family in rented apartments in Washington, Garfield decided to build his own home at a total cost of $13,000. His close friend David G. Swaim (en) lent him half the money.

While Garfield had established himself as an excellent speaker in House debates, he showed little interest in the mood of the members or the ability to control debate on the points he was advancing. He continued to hope for an appointment as chairman of the Ways and Means Committee, but was again disappointed and received the position of chairman of the House Banking Committee (en) but regretted the loss of the Armed Services Committee chairmanship. One of his priorities in this fourth term was legislation to establish a Department of Education; the bill was passed, but its implementation proved difficult due in part to the mismanagement of the Commissioner of Education, Henry Barnard (en).

Garfield also proposed legislation to transfer the Bureau of Indian Affairs from the Interior Department to the War Department. He felt that Native American culture would be more easily "civilized" with the help of a military structure. The proposal was badly received, but Garfield didn't realize it, and the bill was defeated. Garfield was appointed chairman of the census sub-committee, where he reorganized the process and extensively modified the questionnaire. These improvements were presented to the House, which accepted them, but the Senate rejected them. Ten years later, a similar bill was passed, incorporating many of Garfield's ideas.

In September 1870, Garfield was chairman of the congressional committee investigating *Black Friday*, which had seen a spectacular collapse in the gold market on Friday, September 24, 1869. The investigation revealed widespread corruption, but led to no indictments. Garfield refused a subpoena for the president's sister, whose husband was allegedly involved in the scandal, as he considered it irrelevant. He took the opportunity to blame fluctuating greenbacks for the speculation that led to the scandal. Garfield also continued his anti-inflationary campaign against *greenbacks* through his work on a national banking system, and exploited this legislation to reduce the number of *greenbacks* in circulation. Tensions between President Grant and Garfield continued as the committee investigated the accounts of his wife, Julia Grant.

Election of 1870 and fifth term

During the election of 1870, Garfield was criticized, particularly by the steelworkers in his district, for his refusal to implement higher tariffs. On the other hand, merchants criticized his support for tariffs. His opponents accused him of lavish spending on his Washington home, which cost $13,000 when the average cost in his district was $2,000. Nevertheless, his nomination went off without a hitch, and he won the election with almost two-thirds of the vote.

As in his previous terms, Garfield had hoped to secure the chairmanship of the Ways and Means Committee, but once again fell short due to opposition from the influential publisher Horace Greeley. He was appointed Chairman of the Committee on the Appropriation of Public Funds, a position he had previously rejected with contempt. Eventually, this position became his passion, enabling him to improve his management skills. Garfield's view of the Democratic and Republican parties was very negative at the time. He declared that "the death of both parties is almost certain; the Democrats, because all the ideas they have proposed in the last twelve years are dead; and the Republicans, because their ideas have been implemented". Nevertheless, he continued to vote in agreement with his Republican colleagues.

Garfield felt that land grants to the then-expanding railways were unfair. He opposed some of the monopolistic practices of these companies, as well as the powers demanded by the labor unions. By this time, his philosophy on Reconstruction had moderated. He had hailed the passage of the 15th Amendment as a triumph, and favored Georgia's reintegration on constitutional, not political, grounds. In 1871, however, Garfield refused to support the *Ku Klux Klan Act (en)*, declaring: "I have never been more perplexed by any piece of legislation". He was torn between his indignation at "these terrorists" and his concern that the legislation, which authorized the

President to suspend *habeas corpus* to enforce the law, endangered liberties.

Garfield supported the proposal to create a civil service to avoid the many, sometimes aggressive, requests for appointments that elected officials received. In particular, he wanted to eliminate the common practice whereby civil servants paid back part of their salary as "political contributions" in exchange for their appointment.

During his tenure, Garfield became disillusioned with elected office and considered a return to the practice of law; however, he declined an offer of partnership after being warned that his possible partner had a reputation for being "alcoholic and immoral". Garfield was also less willing to sacrifice his family, telling his wife in 1871: "When you are ill, I am like the inhabitants of an earthquake-ravaged country. Like them, I lose faith in the eternal order and immutability of things".

He joins forces with a few other politicians and Jay Cooke's bank to take over the District of Columbia's Public Works Department and embezzle $17 million through fraudulent contracts. Jay Cooke's agent tells him in a cable that "The organization is complete. I still can't believe General Garfield is with us! It's a rare success and most gratifying, as all district contract awards must go through him."

Election of 1872 and sixth term

Garfield was not enthusiastic about Grant's re-election in 1872 until Horace Greeley emerged as the only alternative. His own re-election was virtually unopposed. He was nominated by acclamation and won almost three-quarters of the vote. That same year, he made his first trip west of the Mississippi to sign an agreement for the resettlement of the Têtes-Plates.

In 1872, he was one of many politicians involved in the *Credit Mobilier of America* scandal. As part of their expansion, Union Pacific executives created the *Credit Mobilier of America* and issued shares. These were sold at below-market prices to members of Congress, which was tantamount to bribery as Congress passed several laws to increase the funds paid to Union Pacific. Representative Oakes Ames of Massachusetts certified that Garfield had purchased ten shares of *Credit Mobilier* worth $1,000 and had received $329 (33%) in dividends between December 1867 and June 1868. Ames' credibility was called into question by his numerous reversals under oath and by the lack of evidence he provided. Peskin, Garfield's biographer, wrote: "From a strictly legal point of view, Ames' testimony was worthless. He contradicts himself repeatedly on essential points". According to the *New York Times*, Garfield was in debt and had mortgaged his home. Although Garfield was questioned about the purchase of these shares, he had already returned them to the seller. The scandal did not seriously damage his political career, although he clumsily defended himself against the accusations, as the details were complex and never clearly proven.

On the death of Chief Justice Salmon P. Chase on May 7, 1873. Garfield proposed that he be replaced by Noah H. Swayne (en) but Grant appointed Morrison Waite. Later in his term, Garfield had to vote for a bill from the Committee of Appropriation that included a clause to increase the salaries of Congressmen and the President, which he opposed. This controversial proposal was passed in March 1873, but the violent reaction of the press and public led to its repeal. This vote increased criticism of Garfield, who was nevertheless reappointed chairman of the Committee on Appropriation of Public Funds.

Election of 1874 and seventh term

Garfield and his advisor Harmon Austin saw the need for a more structured campaign organization for the 1874 election. Garfield's appointees volunteered to join his campaign, and his nomination seemed assured. However, he was again accused of corruption in connection with a contract to pave Washington streets by a contractor named DeGolyer McClelland. Contributions of $90,000 to members of Congress, including $5,000 to Garfield, were revealed. He responded to these attacks by precariously stating that these were legal fees obtained through competitive bidding and that technically no federal funds had been used. Several years later, in 1880, correspondence showed that Garfield's influence had been obtained as part of the bidding process. Despite the information available at the time, Garfield put in an excellent performance at the 1874 convention, gathering two-thirds of the delegates before winning the election against the Democratic and Independent candidates, albeit with a smaller lead than before.

The Democrats regained control of Congress in the 1874 election for the first time in 20 years. During the *lame duck session*, Congress passed a compromise measure providing for the reinstatement of metal coinage in 1879. In the new Congress, Garfield was appointed to the Ways and Means Committee and the Pacific Railroad Committee. Garfield and Representative John Coburn (en) of Indiana exposed corruption at the Fort Sill trading post in Oklahoma, where control of supplies had been monopolized and overtaxed. The abuses were corrected by investigation, but Garfield and others were suspected of enabling Secretary of War William W. Belknap to escape prosecution. Belknap to escape prosecution. Belknap later resigned to avoid *impeachment* proceedings when details of his involvement were revealed.

Elections of 1876 and 1878 and last mandates

As the presidential election of 1876 approached, Garfield favored the candidacy of House Speaker James Blaine. However, his health problems and, above all, the revelation of several scandals prevented his nomination in favor of Rutherford B. Hayes; Garfield immediately rallied behind his party's candidate. As far as his own re-election was concerned, Garfield was anxious to leave political life, but faced with his party's difficulties, he felt obliged to stand again. Once again, the nomination was an easy one, and he won 60% of the vote in the election. The party was short-lived, however, as Garfield's youngest child, Neddie, died suddenly of whooping cough.

The presidential election was particularly close, and when it appeared that Republican candidate Rutherford B. Hayes had narrowly lost to Democrat Samuel Jones Tilden, the Republicans set about recounting the votes. Grant asked Garfield to serve as a "neutral observer" at the Louisiana recount. His role soon evolved into investigating *rifle* clubs, which Republicans accused of being created by Democrats to intimidate black voters. Garfield's report and those of other observers cast doubt on the results in Louisiana, South Carolina, Florida and Oregon, which had been marred by widespread fraud on the part of both parties. Since neither candidate had a majority of votes in the Electoral College, the final decision fell, according to the Constitution, to Congress. The latter set up a commission to designate a winner.

Although he opposed the commission, Garfield was appointed to it. Hayes won by 8 votes to 7, and the decision was confirmed despite an attempted filibuster by the Democrats. As James G. Blaine had left the House for the Senate, Garfield became the Republican minority leader in the House.

Garfield ran unopposed for re-election in 1878, despite the presence of a Greenback candidate and redistricting by the Democrats to weaken the Republicans. Garfield garnered 60% of the vote in the election.

Garfield bought a residence in Mentor, Ohio, later renamed Lawnfield by journalists, from which he conducted his "stoop campaign" for the presidency. Today, the house is preserved by the National Park Service as a *James A. Garfield National Historic Site*.

Garfield's last term was largely devoted to confirming Hayes's vetoes of the Democrats' earmarking decisions. With the election-free year of 1879 approaching in Ohio, Garfield sought to secure the Ohio Senate seat vacated by John Sherman upon his appointment as Secretary of the Treasury. The first step was to secure a Republican majority in the Ohio legislature, which would choose the senator. After the Republican victory, Garfield's nomination was no longer in doubt, and he was elected to the Senate by acclamation.

Presidential election of 1880

No sooner had the Ohio legislature chosen Garfield to serve in the Senate in 1879 than a movement began to organize to run him for president the following year, as Hayes wanted to keep his promise of only one term in office. In early 1880, Garfield supported John Sherman's presidential nomination in retribution for Sherman's support of his Senate bid. However, the Republican convention soon reached an impasse, as neither former President Grant, Blaine nor Sherman could gain the upper hand, and delegates began to see Garfield as the candidate of compromise. Garfield eloquently defended West Virginia's dissenting delegates in a speech against Roscoe Conkling's rule that all delegates from the same state must vote for a single candidate. After more than thirty rounds, the proportions of votes cast for the main candidates had barely changed since the start of the convention. In round 34, delegates from several states voted for Garfield, and in round 36, Garfield was chosen as the presidential candidate. Garfield's nomination against the most prominent candidates was considered historic. Garfield defeated front-runner Ulysses S. Grant, who was seeking a third term as president.

Thomas Nichol, Wharton Barker (en) and Benjamin Harrison were considered the main architects of Garfield's rise at the convention, but none could have controlled the unpredictable victory of an *outsider* who had even opposed his candidacy. To win the support of Republican *stalwarts*, former New York harbor customs collector Chester A. Arthur, was chosen to run for Vice-President.

In the wake of such a divisive convention, Garfield's campaign seemed off to a bad start. To heal the divisions, Garfield traveled to New York to bring the warring factions together at the personally successful "New York Conference". It was the only major trip Garfield made away from home during the campaign. The powerful railroads were being courted by the party in the wake of Supreme Court decisions that had gone against their interests. After assuring them that they would have the President's attention on these issues, Garfield won their support.

A major issue in the 1880 election was Chinese immigration. In the West, particularly in California, opponents of Chinese immigration accused it of driving down workers' wages. On the eve of the election, the Democrats published a letter supposedly written by Garfield encouraging Chinese immigration. The timing of the letter's publication, certain inconsistencies and the handwriting itself led many to consider it a forgery.

In the presidential election of 1880, Garfield was pitted against the Democratic candidate Winfield Scott Hancock, another famous Union general. Although Garfield won by 214 electoral votes to 155, the popular vote was the closest in American history, with a margin of just over 7,000 votes out of 8.89 million votes cast. Garfield was also the only president to be elected directly from the House of Representatives, and for a short time he was a sitting representative, senator and president-elect.

Presidency (1881)

Cabinet formation and investiture

Between his election and inauguration, Garfield was busy forming a Cabinet that would ease tensions between Republican Party factions led by Roscoe Conkling and James G. Blaine. Blaine was appointed Secretary of State; the latter was not only the President's closest advisor, he was also obsessed with everything that went on in the White House, and it was said that he even had spies stationed there in his absence. Garfield appointed William Windom of Minnesota as Secretary of the Treasury, William H. Hunt of Louisiana as Secretary of the Navy, Robert Todd Lincoln as Secretary of War and Samuel J. Kirkwood of Iowa as Secretary of the Interior. New York was represented by Thomas L. James as *Postmaster General*. He appointed Wayne MacVeagh of Pennsylvania, an opponent of Blaine's, as Attorney General. Blaine tried to sabotage this choice by convincing Garfield to appoint MacVeagh's enemy, William E. Chandler to the position of Attorney General, which was under MacVeagh's authority. Only the Senate's rejection of Chandler's nomination prevented MacVeagh's resignation.

Garfield's inauguration took place on March 4, 1881 in front of the Capitol in the snow, resulting in an attendance of only 7,000; he was sworn in by Chief Justice Morrison Waite.

In his inaugural address, Garfield emphasized the defense of African-American civil rights. He considered blacks deserving of the "full rights of citizenship" and warned of the danger of blacks' rights being taken away and them becoming a "permanently disenfranchised peasantry". He declared that "liberty can never produce its full benefits so long as law or administration places the smallest obstacle in the way of full citizenship." Garfield argued that those entitled to vote should be able to read and write, and insisted on the need for "universal federal education". On economics, Garfield established that "agreements on bimetallism could be signed between trading nations to secure the general use of both metals". The President championed agriculture as an important part of the American economy, providing "homes and employment for more than half our population and supplying the largest share of our exports". Garfield argued that agricultural science needed federal support. He also declared that polygamy offended the "moral sense of mankind" and that the Church of Jesus Christ of Latter-day Saints, which preached the practice, prevented the "execution of justice through the instrumentality of the law".

Garfield's long struggle for civil service reform was also a focal point of his speech:

"The civil service can never be placed on a satisfactory footing until it is regulated by law. For the good of the service itself, for the protection of those charged with making appointments from the waste of time and obstruction of public business caused by inordinate pressures for positions, and for the protection of serving officials from intrigue and attack."

John Philip Sousa led the *United States Marine Band in the* inaugural parade and ball. The latter was held in the National Museum, now the Arts and Industry Building of Washington's Smithsonian Institution.

Domestic policy

The appointment of Thomas L. James as *Postmaster General* angered Garfield's rival in the Republican Party, the *stalwart* Roscoe Conkling, who demanded a compensatory appointment in favor of his faction and state, and if possible to the Treasury Department. The ensuing feud polluted Garfield's brief presidency. It came to a head when the President, at Blaine's instigation, appointed Conkling's enemy, Judge William H. Robertson (en), to the position of Collector of Customs for the Port of New York. Conkling exploited the principle of "senatorial courtesy" to reject the appointment, but the attempt failed. Garfield, who regarded the practice as cronyism, threatened to cancel all nominations if Robertson's was not accepted. Garfield declared that this would "answer the question whether the President is the Clerk of the Senate or the Chief Executive of the United States". Eventually, Conkling and his colleague Thomas C. Platt resigned their Senate seats in disapproval, but they were further humiliated when the New York legislature chose two others to replace them. Robertson was appointed, and Garfield's victory over the Senate was clear. He had defeated his opponents, weakened the principle of "senatorial courtesy" and strengthened executive power. To Blaine's regret, Garfield returned to his goal of balancing the various party factions and appointed several *stalwarts* close to Conkling to important positions.

Former President Ulysses S. Grant, a Conkling ally, warned Garfield in a letter that he disapproved of Blaine's appointment and was strongly opposed to Robertson's appointment as Collector of Customs for the Port of New York. President Garfield responded with a stern letter in which he wrote that he did not feel bound by party cronyism and that he would appoint "men who represented the best elements of the Republican party".

On July 1, 1881, tensions over the Conkling affair continued as President Garfield continued to deny Vice President Chester A. Arthur, a close associate of Conkling, to Cabinet meetings. Blaine, however, encouraged Garfield in this policy. Historian Justice D. Doenecke argued that Robertson's appointment demonstrated Garfield's lack of judgment. In his opinion, Garfield should have pursued his original policy of conciliating the various Republican factions instead of following Blaine's ideas.

Garfield was responsible for a major economic success when he organized the repayment of $200 million in government loans without calling a special session of Congress. The previous interest rate of 6% was replaced by a future rate of 3.5%, increasing government revenues and limiting the rise in public debt.

Civil service reform

When a new president took office, it was customary for him or her to replace all the officials of the previous administration with party or faction loyalists. This mechanism, known as the spoils system, had been put in place by President Andrew Jackson, but it led to significant corruption and inefficiency in government agencies. Garfield's predecessors had advocated civil service reforms, but no concrete action had been taken.

By 1881, reformist associations had organized across the country and were campaigning energetically. Some reformers were disappointed that Garfield had limited the non-replacement of civil servants to junior positions and had appointed former allies to important posts. Despite this, the majority of reformers remained loyal to Garfield and supported him.

In April 1880, a Congressional investigation revealed a widespread network of corruption within the Post Office Department's *star routes*, which already existed under the Grant and Hayes administrations. Invitations to tender for the management of the postal routes *(star routes),* in full expansion as a result of the conquest of the West, were rigged to favor the most expensive bid, and the profits were then shared between the various parties involved.

Hayes, Garfield's predecessor, halted the implementation of any new postal route contracts in an attempt to stop the corruption. In April 1881, Garfield was informed by Attorney General Wayne MacVeagh and *Postmaster General* Thomas L. James that Second Assistant *Postmaster General* Thomas J. Brady (en) might be one of the main organizers of the corruption. Garfield immediately asked for his resignation and launched investigations that led to a conspiracy trial. When he learned that his party, including his campaign manager Stephen W. Dorsey (en), was involved, Garfield ordered MacVeagh and James to "root out" corruption in the Post Office Department, whatever the consequences. According to the *New York Times*, many alleged members of the corruption were fired or had to resign. Brady had to resign at Garfield's request and was indicted for conspiracy. After two trials, in 1882 and 1883, he was acquitted.

Civil rights

The burden of African-American civil rights weighed heavily on Garfield's presidency. During Reconstruction, freed slaves had been granted citizenship and the right to vote, enabling them to participate in the political life of the country. Garfield felt, however, that their rights had been weakened by white Southern resistance and illiteracy, and he worried about the creation of a "permanent Negro peasantry". The president advocated a federally funded "universal education system" to combat the illiteracy of 70% of Southern blacks. Congress and white Northern public opinion had lost interest in African-American rights, however, and federal funding was rejected by Congress in the 1880s.

Garfield appointed several African-Americans to important positions: Frederick Douglass, Clerk of Deeds in Washington; Robert B. Elliott (en), Special Agent at the Treasury; John M. Langston, Ambassador to Haiti; and Blanche K. Bruce, Clerk of the Treasury. Garfield began to reverse the Southern Democratic policy of conciliation established by Hayes. To strengthen Republican party unity in the South, he appointed William H. Hunt, a Louisiana Republican *carpetbagger* during Reconstruction, as Secretary of the Navy. Garfield believed that the Republican Party could win the support of Southern states on "commercial and industrial" issues rather than racial ones. To break the resurgence of the Democratic Party in the *Solid South*, Garfield tried to favor William Mahone's *Readjuster Party*, whose political positions were popular with both blacks and whites. Garfield thus became the first Republican president to initiate an electoral policy to win the support of Southern independents.

SCENE OF THE ASSASSINATION

Foreign policy

During his short presidency, Garfield appointed several ambassadors, including James Russell Lowell to the UK and Civil War general and *Ben-Hur* author Lewis Wallace to Turkey. Between June 27 and July 1, Garfield appointed 25 ambassadors and consuls, as well as Blaine's son as Third Assistant Secretary of State.

James G. Blaine, Garfield's Secretary of State, was confronted with Chinese immigration, disputes over fishing rights with the U.K. and the recognition of Korea.

Blaine's first task was to put an end to the Pacific War, which had been fought between Chile, Bolivia and Peru since March 5, 1879. In January 1881, Chilean forces captured the Peruvian capital Lima. Rather than remain neutral, Blaine sided with Peruvian leader Francisco García Calderón.

Concerned about potential British intervention, Blaine emphasized the need to settle the conflict between South American states, and invited Peru to pay compensation rather than cede the disputed territory. In November 1881, Blaine sought to organize a conference in Washington with nine South American countries in November 1882. However, these invitations were rescinded in April 1882, when Congress and Arthur cancelled the conference. In October 1883, the Pacific War ended with the Treaty of Ancón without American intervention. Garfield had urged his southern neighbors to strengthen their ties.

As early as 1876, he declared: "I would rather lose five or six diplomatic missions in Europe than those in South America... They are our friends and neighbors". Garfield continued to emphasize the importance of these ties, and campaigned for the Panama Canal to be built by the United States and only under American jurisdiction.

Naval reform

Fifteen years after the American Civil War, the U.S. Navy was in decline. The naval supremacy acquired during the war was fading, and morale was low. Ships were inferior to their European counterparts in terms of firepower, speed and protection. Most American ships were built of wood and iron, and relied on wind power. William H. Hunt, the new Secretary of the Navy, immediately launched an investigation in preparation for a program of reform. A committee headed by Rear Admiral John Rogers called for the construction of 68 new ships, the majority of which were to have iron hulls. Arthur pursued the policy of reform, replacing Hunt with William E. Chandler, an able administrator. Chandler, an able administrator, to continue the modernization program.

His wife's illness

In mid-May 1881, Lucretia Garfield contracted malaria and possibly meningitis. Her temperature reached 40°C and she seemed on the verge of death. By the end of the month, her temperature had dropped and doctors recommended that she recuperate in saline air. Garfield stayed with her during her illness, and on June 18, they left Washington for Elberon, New Jersey, a well-known seaside resort.

After being repeatedly rebuffed, Charles J. Guiteau, a troubled lawyer and *stalwart* supporter in search of a government job, decided to assassinate the president. After purchasing a revolver, Guiteau tracked Garfield to Lafayette Square Park and his Disciples of Christ Church in Washington. Learning that Garfield was going to Elberon on June 18, Guiteau decided to assassinate him at the Washington train station. He decided not to shoot, however, because of his wife's fragile health, which he did not wish to burden.

While his wife recuperated in the cool ocean air, President Garfield convened his Cabinet in Elberon and governed by telegraph. While staying at the Elberon Hotel, the President reviewed the 7th Infantry Regiment and interacted with the journalists present. Garfield was also scheduled to attend a banquet honoring the city's veterans, but opted to withdraw after learning that his

80-year-old uncle, Thomas Garfield, had been killed in a locomotive accident in Cleveland, Ohio. Former President Grant, who had traveled with his family to Elberon, met Garfield informally on June 25. After attending mass, Garfield returned to Washington the following day, June 27, 1881.

Administration and judicial appointments

Despite his short presidency, Garfield appointed a Supreme Court Justice: Stanley Matthews (en) to replace the retiring Noah H. Swayne. In addition to this appointment, Garfield named four judges to lower courts: Don Albert Pardee (en) to the Court of Appeals for the Fifth Circuit (where he remained until 1919), Alexander Boardman (en) to the District Court of Western Louisiana, Addison Brown to the District Court for the Southern District of New York and LeBaron B. Colt (en) to the District Court of Rhode Island.

Murder

On the morning of July 2, 1881, President Garfield went to Williams College, where he had studied, to give a speech. He was accompanied by James G. Blaine, Robert Todd Lincoln and his two sons, James and Harry. As the president crossed the street to the Baltimore and Potomac Railroad station in Washington at 9:30 a.m., Charles J. Guiteau approached Garfield and shot him twice in the back at point-blank range. Garfield was upset that his application to become consul in Paris had been turned down several times because he had no qualifications. He suffered from mental problems and was convinced that he had given a speech that was decisive in Garfield's election. When his nomination was rejected, Guiteau began to believe that the Republican party and the country had been betrayed, and that God had told him he could save the nation and the party if Garfield was "eliminated". Guiteau followed the president for weeks with a Webley Bulldog revolver. Upon his arrest, he cried out "I am the *stalwart* of the *stalwarts...* Arthur is now President!". This led to rumors, quickly dismissed, that Arthur or his supporters had urged Guiteau to act. Guiteau also assumed that he would be acquitted and elected president after his trial.

Garfield cried out immediately after being hit: "My God, what's that? The first bullet grazed Garfield's arm and the second lodged near his liver, but the doctors were unable to locate it precisely; the autopsy revealed that it was behind the pancreas.

Alexander Graham Bell developed a metal detector to find the famous bullet in the President's body, but interference from the iron-framed bed prevented the device from working. Garfield's condition deteriorated sharply in the following weeks, as the infection weakened his heart. He remained bedridden at the White House, suffering from fevers and severe pain. To relieve the wounded man from the sweltering Washington summer heat, naval engineers developed one of the first air-conditioning devices. Fans forced air through a crate full of ice into the President's room. The system worked satisfactorily, lowering the temperature by about ten degrees Celsius.

Messages of support arrived from all over the country and the world. King Humbert I of Italy and the Rothschild family sent messages of condolence, and Kentucky's Democratic Governor Luke P. Blackburn ordered a day of "public fasting and prayer". While Article II, Clause 6 of the Constitution provided that in the event of the President's "inability to exercise the powers and perform the duties of his office", these fell to the Vice-President,

Chester A. Arthur was reluctant to act as President while Garfield was still alive, and the next two months saw a vacuum with Garfield too weak to carry out his duties, and Arthur refusing to assume them. However, federal activities were fairly limited during the summer period and the President had few missions to carry out, so this did not result in a major crisis.

On September 6, Garfield was taken to the New Jersey shore in the faint hope that the fresh air might help his recovery. Within hours, locals were building a rail spur for Garfield's train.

On Monday, September 19, 1881, at 10:20 p.m., Garfield died of a myocardial infarction or ruptured splenic artery aneurysm, following sepsis and pneumonia. Garfield was pronounced dead at 10:35 p.m. in Elberon. Lucretia stayed with her husband for an hour until she was escorted from the room. He died exactly two months before his fiftieth birthday, making him the second youngest president to be assassinated during his term of office, after John Fitzgerald Kennedy. In the 80 days between the assassination attempt and his death, his only official act was to sign an extradition document. His last words were "My work is done".

Today, most historians and medical experts believe that Garfield would probably have survived his wounds had his doctors had access to current techniques and operating procedures. As the medical practice of the time advised, several doctors attempted to retrieve the bullet from Garfield's body, but did so with their fingers, or with unsterilized instruments, causing the then incurable septicemia. Joseph Lister's work on sterilization in the 1860s was not yet fully accepted by American physicians, and historians agree that infection was one of the main causes of Garfield's death. Nevertheless, biographer Peskin argues that the wound was so severe that, even without infection, it would have been fatal.

Guiteau was formally charged with Garfield's murder on October 14, 1881. Despite his insanity defense, the jury sentenced him to death on January 5, 1882, and he was hanged on June 30.

Heritage

1,500 people gathered in front of Garfield's coffin in Elberon before he was taken away in a hearse. His body was taken by train to Washington, and thousands of onlookers lined the tracks. More than 70,000 people, some of whom had waited for three hours, paraded in front of his coffin in Washington, and on September 25, 1881, more than 150,000 people, outnumbering the city's population, paid their last respects in Cleveland. Garfield's body was placed in a specially designed building, lit by electricity, and a wreath sent by Queen Victoria of the United Kingdom adorned his coffin.

His body was temporarily placed in a vault in Cleveland's Lake View Cemetery before his memorial was erected.

On May 18, 1887, the monument to James A. Garfield (en) was unveiled in Washington. The monument consists of a 3 m-high bronze statue of Garfield, placed atop a 5 m-high Baroque-style plinth, and stands in front of the U.S. Capitol. Three 5-m bronze allegorical figures placed at the base of the plinth represent the three important periods in Garfield's life: student, soldier and statesman.

On May 19, 1890, Garfield's body was laid to rest with full honors in a mausoleum at Lake View Cemetery in Cleveland, Ohio. Former President Rutherford B. Hayes, sitting President Benjamin Harrison and future President William McKinley attended the dedication. President Harrison declared that Garfield was still "a student and a teacher" and that his work would live on after his death. Five panels of the monument depict Garfield as a teacher, as a Union general, as an orator, during his swearing-in ceremony, and his coffin in the Capitol rotunda.

There were two years in which the United States had three presidents. The first was 1841. Martin Van Buren completed his sole term on March 4, William Henry Harrison was inaugurated, but died a month later before his vice-president John Tyler succeeded him. The second was 1881. Rutherford B. Hayes was succeeded by James A. Garfield. Garfield and, on the latter's death, Chester A. Arthur became president.

The assassination of President Garfield by a disturbed man in search of a government job shook public opinion, and Congress embarked on civil service reform.

Democratic Senator George H. Pendleton of Ohio proposed legislation that was signed into law by President Arthur in January 1883. The *Pendleton Civil Service Reform Act* introduced competitive examinations for civil service and merit-based appointments. The law outlawed the common practice of paying or rendering services to obtain an appointment. To enforce the reform, Congress created the *Civil Service Commission*. The *Pendleton Act* initially covered only 10% of federal positions, but successive reforms meant that by the early 20th century, the vast majority of federal appointments were made on the basis of merit. President Arthur, who had a reputation as a supporter of the spoils system, became a strong advocate of this reform.

However, nothing was done to provide close protection for the President. It was only after the assassination of William McKinley, twenty years later, that Congress entrusted the *Secret Service,* originally founded to combat counterfeiting, with the President's security.

In 1876, Garfield demonstrated his mathematical talents with a proof of the Pythagorean theorem. His work was published in the *New England Journal of Education*. Mathematics historian William Dunham commented that Garfield's demonstration was "a very elegant proof indeed".

The Australian town of Garfield, formerly known as Cannibal Creek, took its name in honor of the late president in 1887, and his effigy was printed on $20 gold certificates and $5 bills issued in 1882.

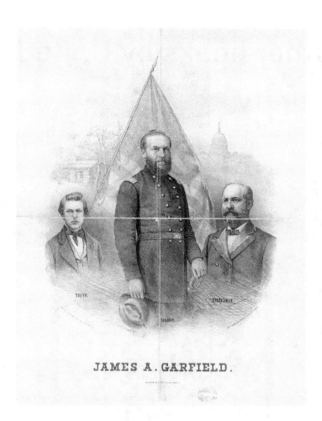

JAMES A. GARFIELD.

Other books by United Library

https://campsite.bio/unitedlibrary

9 789464 903232